Caroline Righton's

CREATE IT
WITH
THREAD
IN AN
EVENING

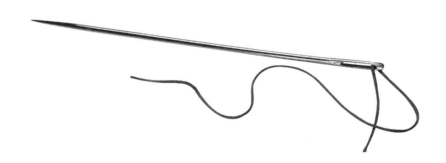

NEXUS SPECIAL INTERESTS

Caroline Righton's

CREATE IT
— WITH —
THREAD
— IN AN —
EVENING

DESIGNER
ELAINE DONOVAN
PHOTOGRAPHER
RICHARD LAING

Caroline Righton's

NEXUS SPECIAL INTERESTS

Nexus Special Interests Ltd.
Nexus House
Azalea Drive
Swanley
Kent BR8 8HU
England

First published in Great Britain by Nexus Special Interests Ltd., 1998

ISDN 1-85486-176-X

**Dedicated to Scilla Grose, Suzy Pass and Ann Marchetti
with gratitude**

Colour separations by PDQ, Bungay, Suffolk
Printed and bound in Great Britain by Jarrold Book Printing, Thetford, Norfolk

CONTENTS

INTRODUCTION

Life today can be so hectic that spare time is all the more precious and while it would be easy to spend that spare time catching up on the domestic chores or doing extra shopping, I bet you wish you could just take a bit of time out for you occasionally and lose yourself in something absorbing and creative.

The trouble is - by the time you've got yourself organised to do anything productive it's time to stop again and you have to leave it half finished because of all the other demands on your time.

Well this book is for you - all the craft ideas in it are 'do-able' in a few hours. Believe me I've done them! If you add a call to your local craft store or artists' suppliers shop to your supermarket dash, then by the end of the day you should have created something for yourself, your home or as a gift. More importantly you will have spent a lovely creative evening, which has relaxed you and certainly taken your mind off the million and one other things your children, your partner, your boss etc. want you to worry about.

Creating something in an evening with thread offers you a million and one possibilities. This book has nine projects that involve some really traditional sewing techniques and stitches such as quilting and embroidery, but also has ideas about how to be creative with your sewing machine if you have one. So first of all, decide how you feel. For example, do you fancy sitting in your armchair with half an eye on the telly while you do some cross-stitch or tapestry? Or would you rather clear a large area, cut out patterns in different fabrics and appliqué a tablecloth? Or perhaps you would like to get out the sewing machine and whizz up a quickie patchwork cushion cover. The choice is yours! Have fun!

7

THREAD

There are nine different projects in this book using thread...all of them easily achievable in an evening.

APPLIQUE

Appliqué might seem to you to have rather naive connotations and often people confuse it with the craft of collage where elements are placed together to make a picture. Some of the principles of appliqué are the same, but don't be deceived by its childlike simplicity because it really is one of the most effective and quick ways to achieve stunning effects and cover a large area using fabric and thread. Using appliqué on a broad canvas is the project to make a snakes and ladders playmat, which can have absolutely minimal stitching and be done either by machine or hand. The crisp summery tablecloth makes creative use of the machine, and the individual tablemat and napkin set uses only hand stitching and embroidery.

EMBROIDERY, TAPESTRY AND CROSS-STITCH

It might seem crazy to lump together these three very different types of needlecraft stitchery into one section of the book but the projects covered do all have one particular thing in common - they are all dependent on the stitchcraft of you and your needle. People do have particular inclinations to types of sewing so I wanted to offer something for the main ones. We all know how wonderful it is spending time doing some stitching but it is easy to feel daunted embarking on big projects. I am offering you three things to make using different types of stitching that can be completed in just a few hours.

PATCHWORK AND QUILTING

Is there anyone who firstly, doesn't like the idea of patchwork and secondly, who doesn't respond to the look and feel of quilting? The problem with both as crafts to enjoy, in my experience, is that they take quite a lot of organisation to do and then need the sort of attention to detail that requires the amount of time that I just don't ever seem to have!

So it was quite a challenge to come up with three projects using patchwork and quilting that I felt you could happily tackle and achieve in an evening. However, by taking a modern approach to a very old needlecraft I hope you'll agree the tablemat, evening purse and, of course, the cushion offer the perfect solutions.

APPLIQUE

I hope the three appliqué projects I have chosen show the different effects and styles you can achieve.

I have chosen these three projects because they will introduce you to the basic techniques of laying out and securing designs - then, of course, you can do your own patterns. Traditional appliqué designs are quite simple but the more practiced you become the more adventurous and detailed you can make your work.

The snakes and ladders project uses many different items and textiles to 'apply' in many different ways. It is very easy to get carried away and I must admit completing it all in an evening will require some 'applique-ation'! Still have a go and see how you get on.

T H E   O R I G I N S   O F   A P P L I Q U E

The word appliqué comes from the French verb 'to put on' and it's defined by London's Victoria and Albert Museum as 'the sewing of patches to the surface of a material so they form a pattern either by their own shape and colour, or by the shape and colour of the ground material'.

As a craft it has had its place in almost every culture's history where different pieces of fabric are stitched onto a backing cloth to create a picture or design that often reflects and illustrates the times in which it has been made.

Often different stitches are used as part of a design incorporating other objects such as buttons, scraps of metal or even tiny cymbals or bells. These may have special meanings such as in the arid parts of India where tiny mirrors are sewn onto fabric and represent the importance of water in these regions.

India, in fact, is where much of the best appliqué work can be found. In northern India, in particular, the craft has been elevated to a real art form and Rajasthani appliqué uses folded and cut pieces of material while different communities in the Kutch region portray and parade their individual tribal identities through their appliquéd costumes which they also embroider elaborately. Often a family's wealth can be indicated by the quality and richness of their decorated wardrobe.

Another Eastern country where appliqué is important is Thailand where, in fact, these sewing skills are so valued that there is a wonderful myth about how the earth was created by a needlewoman who sewed the lands together and pulled up the mountains with her needle. In some areas a woman's prestige depends on her sewing skills which are demonstrated particularly in the White and Blue Meo hill tribes costumes of appliquéd belts and collars.

In the West appliqué was used as far back as the thirteenth and fourteenth centuries on velvet and silks in church embroidery for monasteries. These works often used linen shapes, which were carefully stitched separately using real gold and silver threads, and were then cut out and applied to the precious fabrics. The edges would be either couched or braided, often with a padded satin stitch. Another way was to apply the patches worked on linen, to cut wide of the outline and then fray it back to the stitching using the frayed ends of thread to stitch it securely into place.

Appliqué and quilting go hand in hand and along with India, another great cotton-producing nation, the USA, has played its part in the history of the craft. American cotton was popular in the making of the warm padded quilts of the eighteenth and nineteenth centuries. When the American cottons reached Hawaii appliqué was used to combine vibrant colours and create designs often inspired by leaves or fruit. These cut pieces would come from a single piece of fabric laid on a plain backing cloth. So important are these pieces in the area's history that they have been given special names such as the Comb of Kaiuland or Garden Island.

Today appliqué is very popular and Oriental, European, American and Caribbean influences can all be seen on clothing and in furnishings. New designs are always being rediscovered and created. An example of how ancient appliqué designs have prompted a modern fashion trend is the effect a display of blouses from the Kuna people of a group of islands near the coast of Pananma had on the craft in America in the 1960s. The blouses of their traditional costumes are heavily appliquéd and have cut worked mola panels on them. Mola is the Kuna word for cloth, and in a small space the needlewomen of the islands seemed able to incorporate a dazzling array of cut pieces, patched pieces and intricate stitchery. Nothing like them had ever been seen before by the outside world. A national magazine produced a feature on them and 'mola making' or 'reverse appliqué' became a fashion and craft craze in the States.

Mola making is a perfect example of the variety of items created through the history of appliqué. While many people turn to the craft today because it is a quick effective way to decorate a large piece of fabric, the intricate work a traditional mola blouse requires can take up to two years to complete.

Background fabric

Contrasting material

Wadding

Interesting buttons, sequins etc.

Scissors

Pinking shears

Paper for templates

Pencil

Needle

Sewing machine

Thread for machine and
  embroidery

Glue for fabric or PVA

Bondaweb

Iron

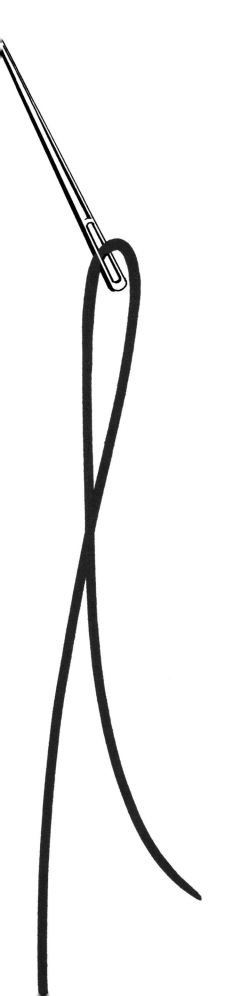

E Q U I P M E N T

The equipment you need for appliqué is the same as you would need for most sewing projects.

You start with your basic **background fabric** and then choose some **contrasting material.** This does not have to be in large quantities and good use can be made of interesting scraps. It helps if both can be of the same weight and type of fabric, especially if the item will require regular washing.

You will need **pencil and paper** to mark out and make templates and a good sharp pair of scissors for cutting out. **Pinking shears** will save you hours of hemming and overcasting. **Dressmaker's pins** will be needed to position your designs and help make the designing process more fluid.

A medium **needle** and suitable all-purpose **thread** should be the basic tools for hand sewing, but you may wish to try different needles for heavier thread. When using a **sewing machine** you can use straight stitching or set it to a narrow zigzag stitch.

If you are applying larger pieces of fabric then you could use **PVA glue** or **Bondaweb** - an iron-on web adhesive which is easy to use and is a wee bit faster than hand sewing! This means you can use your embroidery skills to decorate rather than secure.

Of course a good **iron** is a must as all materials should be 'crease free' before attaching and then the finished item will need a good ironing on completion.

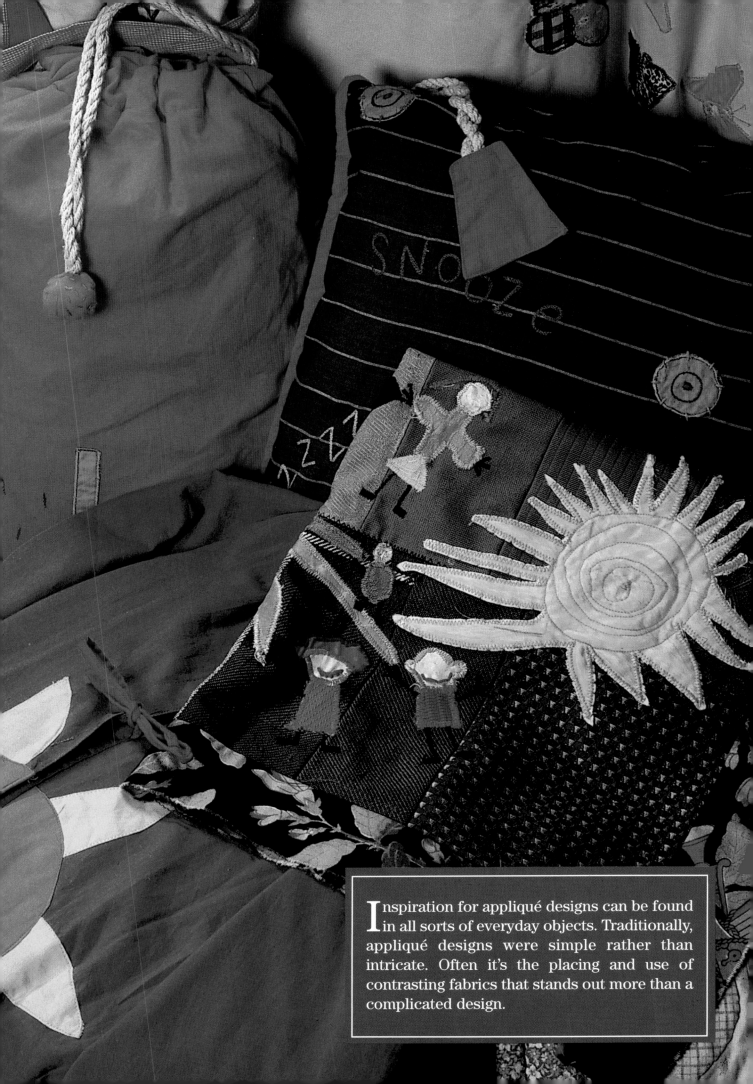

Inspiration for appliqué designs can be found in all sorts of everyday objects. Traditionally, appliqué designs were simple rather than intricate. Often it's the placing and use of contrasting fabrics that stands out more than a complicated design.

TECHNIQUES

The most important thing to get right in appliqué is your initial design. Look around for simple images that you like. Children's books are excellent sources of inspiration for clear shapes and colours. Start with a basic shape and then build up the details with different fabrics and textures.

MAKING THE TEMPLATE AND TRACING

Unless your design is very 'free style' you will need to make patterns to cut out all the pieces of fabric. The simplest method is to find a shape or design you like in a book or magazine and trace over it - you can enlarge or reduce it to the size you want on a photocopier. Then cut out the shape and if it is to be used many times re-cut it from thin card. You will then have to make separate tracings of any details on your design so you can cut them out separately too.

STICKING AND BONDAWEB

The step-by-step instructions explain all about stitching your appliqué pieces which is the traditional way to secure your stitches, but I'm a great believer in using whatever methods you can if time is at a premium and a great invention has to be fusing web. This comes as a fine sheet and is, in essence, a bonding agent that holds two pieces of fabric together when it is melted between them. It works best on large pieces and most of the products on the market will hold during normal cleaning. You need to cut out an identical shape and pin it to the wrong side of the fabric. Pin the appliqué and web to the right side of the background, making sure they are perfectly aligned, and then heat fix by pressing lightly with an iron to anchor it and then again with an iron over a damp cloth. Do check the manufacturer's instructions. I also occasionally use fabric glue which works well but is a bit messier than fusing web.

LAYERING

Appliqué made up of several over lapping layers looks really great and there are some simple techniques that you can use to make sure you don't get in a muddle. Make a plan of your design and number each piece from the lowest layer up to the tiniest top detail. Then remove all the pieces except for the first bottom ones which you should secure first. You won't need to worry too much about the edges that are going to be covered by other layers and, in fact, to hem or stitch them would make them show through later layers. Once the bottom piece is secure you can then carry on placing the overlapping layers until you get to the point of just adding detail and top stitches.

ADDING EXTRA OBJECTS

Try to keep an open mind about your appliqué. Because we are trying to make a completed item in just one evening you can cover a lot of ground by replacing whole areas of embroidery with the application of some imaginative substitutes and I don't think your work will be at all diminished by doing so. For instance this stitched raffia works better and gives more added interest to the hen's nest than several hours of stem-stitching could ever have done. The flower button works brilliantly as the bird's beady eye.

STEP-BY-STEP

CHOOSING MATERIALS

The first thing you need to do is to decide upon your backing fabric. It may be an exciting item such as a rug, tablemat or cushion cover. It's worth properly considering this blank canvas for a little time. For example, for my tablecloth project when I decided to stitch together some different fabrics for the backing base to add even more interest. Now decide on your design and theme and choose the contrasting fabrics, other items and threads that you are going to use. Place them overlapping on the base fabric so you can get an idea how they will work together.

MAKING THE TEMPLATE AND CUTTING OUT YOUR DESIGN

Draw the outline of your design on some plain paper and cut it out. Pin this to a piece of fabric and cut around it. Place it on your base fabric. Before you start to do any sewing make all the paper patterns and cut out all the different pieces of fabric you plan to use, and lay them on your piece so you can decide on the final look before you start securing it. Believe me this is the only way - I nearly always end up changing my mind about the layout at this stage.

SECURING YOUR FABRIC

Traditionally you should pin and then tack your pieces in place using a large running stitch, but as explained in 'techniques', you can also use fabric glue or bondaweb, layering the fabric as you proceed. You may need to make a small hem on each piece where the fabric is quick to fray. My advice is try to avoid those fabrics and always use pinking shears. The most important thing to remember is always make sure each piece is well ironed and work up from the base piece which is likely to be the largest.

20

STITCHES

It is really the stitches used in appliqué that make it so interesting to do and add the finishing touch, although the playmat project shows that if your needle skills only extend to a running stitch on the sewing machine, gluing your layers can be just as effective in some cases.

You should choose your thread according to the style and type of your piece but remember that the sewing is not just functional - it is there to be very visible and add something decorative to the item. I like to use contrasting embroidery silks, threaded as thickly as the fabric will allow.

BLANKET-STITCH

CHAIN-STITCH

SATIN-STITCH

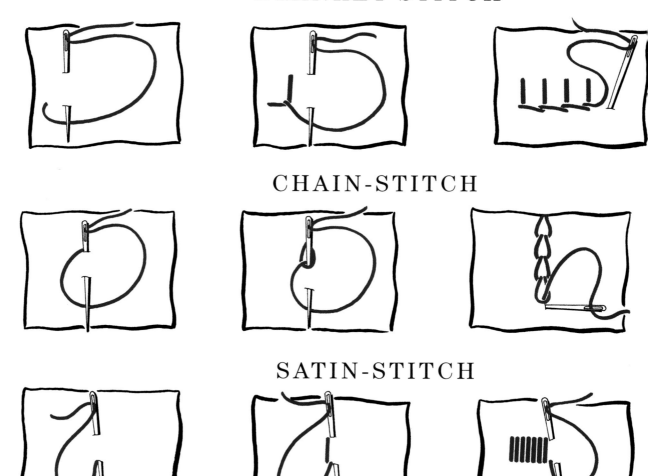

The most traditional appliqué stitch to hold down your fabric pieces and make a neat edge and outline is blanket-stitch.

Chain-stitch is an excellent defining stitch because it can make a line of significant weight, thickness and interesting texture

Satin-stitch is really effective for pulling together several corners of fabric as in the flower centres on my tablecloth.

If you want to use your machine only for appliqué then a simple running stitch or zigzag stitch will work perfectly for both hemming and securing raw edges.

SNAKES AND LADDERS PLAYMAT

YOU WILL NEED

Checked material that is cut 10 squares each side with an extra 2cm seam allowance
round the edge

Contrasting quilting backing cloth

Scissors

Two colours - 2.5 metres of bias binding

Two colours - 1 metre of thin ribbon

Several different coloured squares of felt

Felt numbers from your children's fuzzy felt sets

Pins

Paper and pens

Fabric pens

Bit of paper

Scissors for paper

Rubber snakes

Glue/Bondaweb

This project is all sticking and fusing appliqué leaving the option up to you whether to add stitches or not. Once you have filled in your hundred squares, place it right sides together with the quilted backing, sew along the seam allowance on three sides, turn right sides out and then hand-stitch the remaining edge.

SNAKES AND LADDERS PLAYMAT

This is great fun to make. Put in as much detail as you have time to do. I drew the snakes and numbers freehand on the felt squares, making sure to do the numbers back to front so the pen marks didn't show. Raid the children's toy boxes for snakes, ladders etc.

P A T T E R N

Y O U   W I L L   N E E D

- A copy of this pattern photocopied and enlarged as necessary
- Tablemat
- Napkins
- Scraps of material
- Embroidery cotton - colours to suit
- Embroidery needle
- Raffia
- Green binca for grass
- Felt
- Button for eye
- Scissors

HEN AND EGG TABLEMAT
AND NAPKIN

Great fun at breakfast especially for the younger members of the family.
"And what does Mr. Hen say if you don't eat all your egg?"

T A B L E C L O T H

Y O U   W I L L   N E E D

Tablecloth

Scraps of materials

Embroidery cotton

Needle

Coloured ribbon

Pinking shears

Scissors

I didn't use a pattern because I wanted it quickly for a picnic the next day and risked free-style cutting out of the flower petals. It's all machine appliqué apart from the satin-stitched flower centres.

TABLECLOTH

I love table linen but it seems to fall into two categories - white and for best or beautifully fashionable and colourfully stylish - and still an expensive purchase on the basis it may be last year's look next summer. Here's the perfect solution - make your own.

WHY STOP THERE?

when there are so many other plain items around your home that could
be cheered up with a little application of appliqué?

EMBROIDERY

Stitching projects are, more often than not, long-term projects. I'm renowned for starting a needlepoint cushion cover in the autumn, which I plan to stitch through the long evenings of winter and have completed by spring. My friend Suzy is working on several large cross-stitch pieces at once and some have been on the go for years.

But the three projects in this section of the book allow you to choose the sort of stitch you want to do and then produce a finished item by the end of an evening.

The Chinese symbols of happiness and good luck in cross-stitch are very straightforward - the key fob loses none of its individuality for being quick to make and the embroidery sampler with a difference allows for freedom of expression and a bit of individual creativity while experimenting with different stitches.

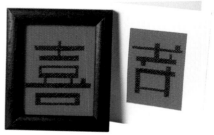

31

THE ORIGINS OF EMBROIDERY

I suppose it must have been cavemen that invented embroidery when they joined two animal skins together to make bedding and clothing. Weaving developed with linen in the Middle East and silk in the Far East, and that makes it difficult to say where embroidery as we know it today started. It seems to have developed simultaneously in the Far and Middle East. In ancient Egypt it was seen on tomb paintings, and Greek embroidery on quilts was to be found on vase paintings.

The earliest surviving example of stitchcraft on fabric is Scythian and dates back to the 3rd century BC.

The Chinese have made it an art form and Chinese embroidery can be traced back to the Tang dynasty AD 618-907, with the most opulent period being the Manchu dynasty with its imperial silk robes.
It is thought that the influence of designs and skills was a two-way process moving from the Middle East to Afghanistan, China and India where men were the expert embroiderers.

Work started to be imported to Europe in the 1550s from India, and these designs influenced English embroidery, as did the imports by the Dutch East India Company in the 16th and 17th centuries.

Embroidery had its home in ecclesiastical vestments. In Britain secular embroidery developed in Henry VIII's reign and was fully recognised by Elizabeth I with the grant of charter to the Broderers Company. It is thought that Elizabeth I and Mary Queen of Scots were both excellent needlewomen, and might well have been influenced by Catherine of Aragon who is thought to have introduced new stitches from the continent.

English and French styles began to merge in the 16th century and became very similar. Work and new designs became more decorative and less useful, and the 17th century saw the introduction of pattern books, needlepoint and samplers.

In the Americas embroidery reflected its tapestry of immigrant cultures. In South America the influence was Hispanic whereas North American embroidery followed the European style, although the designs tended to be simpler. As in Europe, the practical gave way to decorative, and samplers and embroidered pictures were popular.

Berlin woolwork introduced in the 19th century, almost made embroidery extinct. It became so popular because of the introduction of new softer wool and aniline dyes, which made highly detailed and colourful work possible to copy by charting.

However, the Royal School of Needlework, founded in 1872 and the Embroiderers Guild established in the 1920s have maintained and nurtured traditional skills. Embroidery has seen a revival in popularity in the 1960s and 70s with the renewed interest in handicrafts and the advent of kits containing all you require to complete a project.

Threads

Hoops and frames

Needles

Dressmaking shears

Embroidery scissors

Dressmaker's pencil

Tape measure

Thimbles

Needle threader

Sewing machine

Thread for machine

T-pins

Magnifier

Blocking board

Iron

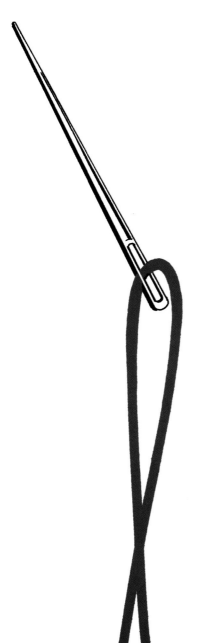

EQUIPMENT

Many of you will have the basic equipment needed for embroidery
You start with your basic **background fabric** which will come from one
of three categories: **plain weave** like **linen, even weave** like **binca
cloth** and **surface-patterned material** such as **gingham.**

A large number of effects can be achieved with embroidery and you can
use lots of different types of **thread**. In **wool** there is **crewel, Persian,
rug and tapestry wool**, and there is a multitude of embroidery silks to
choose from.

You can use **an embroidery frame or hoop** to keep the material
stretched while you sew.

A good selection of **needles** will be required and the ones you use will
depend on your project. There are many different types and they come
in a range of different sizes. The bigger the number the smaller the
needle.

A sharp pair of small **embroidery scissors** is important as well as a pair
of **cutting out scissors**. Other useful things are a **tape measure**, a
needle threader and a **thimble**. You may also find useful a **ruler,
magnifier** (for close work), and **masking tape.**

If you are artistic and want to attempt your own designs then you will
need marking and **transfer pencils** plus **dressmakers' carbon** and
tracing papers to transfer your design to the material.

Y ou have to think beyond the stitches to enjoy embroidery as a craft to do in an evening and take a view on the impact your project is going to have.

Make the most of the stitches you can do in the time you have got and most of all - enjoy yourself!

TECHNIQUES

There are lots of tips and techniques that will help you enjoy whatever type of sewing you decide to take up but many of these will only be appropriate to one particular needle skill. Those I list here are ones that are common to all three disciplines; cross-stitch, canvas or wool work.

You can use an embroidery hoop which will hold your fabric taut while you are stitching it. They come in different shapes and sizes and are made from wood or plastic with a screw on the outer ring to allow you to adjust the fit. When the fabric is taut enough it should feel like a drum when tapped.

You should work with thread no longer than 50cm and separate the number of strands you need.

Threading a needle should be the easiest thing in the world but it can be a nightmare start to your project if you can't get the wretched thread through the eye - buy a needle threader which will solve this particular problem in a second.

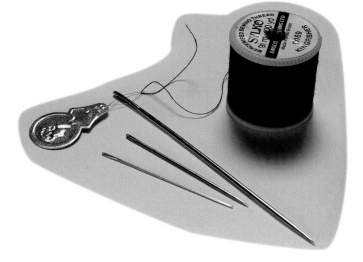

Leave a couple of centimetres of thread at the back of your first stitch for catching in with the first couple of stitches to secure. If your thread becomes twisted and kinked while you are sewing just hold your fabric upside down and let the thread and needle dangle until it has unwound itself (this trick works with telephone leads too!).

As you come to the end of your piece of thread take your needle and thread through the back of some stitches to make a neat and tidy finish.

If you feel ambitious enough to try to create your own designs then the simplest way is to get some graph paper and literally treat each square as a stitch, colouring it in the appropriate colour. Then you can count your threads on your fabric and recreate it. If you get really fired up by this idea and have a computer you can buy programmes that will turn photographs into stitch charts.

You can also buy hot iron transfers, which are especially useful for cross-stitch. In fact, my earliest memory of embroidery is watching my mother iron the blue transfers onto a tray cloth she planned to stitch. A friend of mine swears by them for cross-stitch in particular, although cross-stitch is so much about counting threads that I prefer not to use them. The thing to do is to experiment and find the way that suits you best.

Finally, a finishing tip if your work has got grubby during the making. Check that all your sewing threads are washable and colourfast (I'm speaking here as someone who ruined a three-month embroidery when the colours all ran as I washed it!) and then gently squeeze it in tepid soapy water - you can actually buy special embroidery washing powder. Then rinse it a couple of times and roll it in a towel to blot the excess water. If the threads aren't washable take it to a dry cleaner.

STEP-BY-STEP

Although some professional embroiderer friends of mine have said I must be mad to try to tell you how to carry out three embroidery disciplines in short step-by-step instructions, in their simplest form the principles for all three are pretty similar. However, if you find yourself becoming enthusiastic for one particular discipline then do find out all the intricacies of the skill relevant to that particular type of sewing.

The first thing is to consider your basic material. To work with wool on a project such as the key fob you will need an open-weave fabric or canvas. Other embroidery skills, such as cross-stitch, can be done on many different sorts of fabric, although the beginner will probably find it easiest to work on an even-weave fabric where the number of threads per square centimetre is the same up and down. You will probably remember binca cloth from school. Well, as an adult you should be looking for a finer weave although the principle is the same. Be adventurous if you dare, especially for the sampler, because it is the use of silk as the base fabric that makes the piece so special. Next choose the thread and needle that is appropriate for the fabric you are going to work.

Unsurprisingly embroidery is all about the stitches, so the major part of these step-by- step instructions are concerned with those in particular.

For canvas work, your best bet is to use tent-stitch. This forms an even texture applicable to almost any type of design and can be used with toning coloured wool to give a shading effect. Tent-stitch is also more hardwearing than other stitches although it does use up more thread.

TENT-STITCH

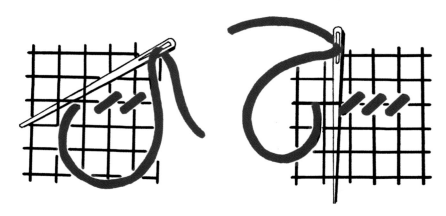

Cross-stitch is really a variation on a theme. As the name implies a cross-stitch involves making the threads cross. It's probably the best-known embroidery stitch and the one you are most likely to have learnt at school. You can either work stitch by stitch, or you can stitch one row of diagonals and then go back over it making the crosses.

CROSS-STITCH

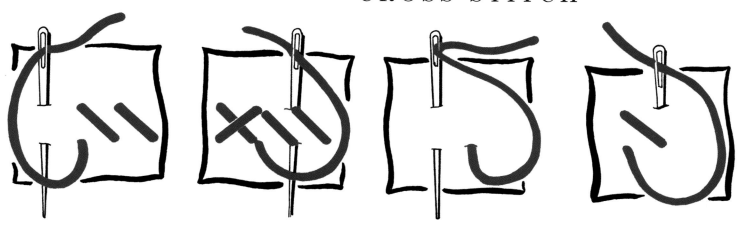

Other well-known embroidery stitches you will find useful in your sewing include:

LAZY DAISY

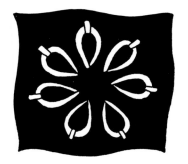

BACK-STITCH

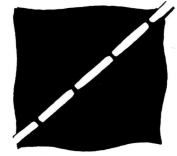

FRENCH KNOT

STEM-STITCH

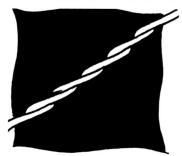

When you have finished your piece you must press it to remove any wrinkles. Put a towel on your ironing board, lay down your piece, cover it with a damp cloth and press very lightly with a warm iron.

PATTERN

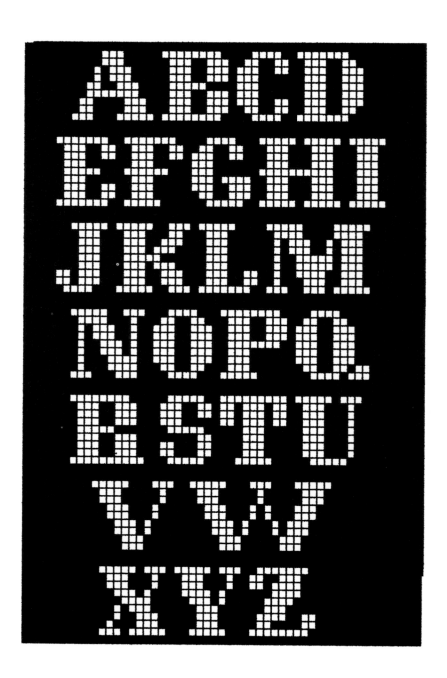

YOU WILL NEED

- 10-mesh canvas
- Backing fabric such as felt or velvet
- Stuffing material
- Metal keyring (if required)

- Tapestry wool
- Tapestry needle
- Cord and tassel

Use 1/2 tent stitch. Fold canvas in half to mark the middle and count out stitches of the letter either side to centre it. Follow pattern and elaborate if you want to personalise it. Fill in background and do border. Stitch together the canvas with the felt, right side in, on three sides. Pull right side out and stuff. Hand stitch 4th side and sew on cord and tassel.

K E Y   F O B

This key fob may be too big to carry around with you in your pocket, but it is ideal for identifying individual household keys or for a special jewellery or memento box

P A T T E R N

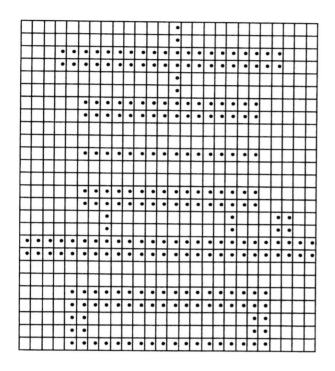 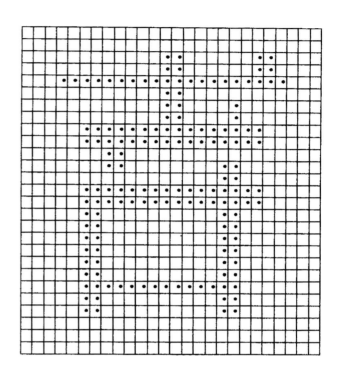

YOU WILL NEED

- Template
- Black standard embroidery cotton
- Binca
- Frame
- Card
- Needles

These are really simple to do - mind you, if you get a stitch wrong who knows what the message might mean!

CHINESE CROSS-STITCH

I downloaded these symbols from a Chinese dictionary on the Internet.
One means 'happiness' and the other 'good luck'.
Stitch them and turn them into cards, pictures, a pin cushion etc. and
give them as gifts.

PATTERN

Most of the stitches are explained on pages 40 and 41 but other stitches I have used here include

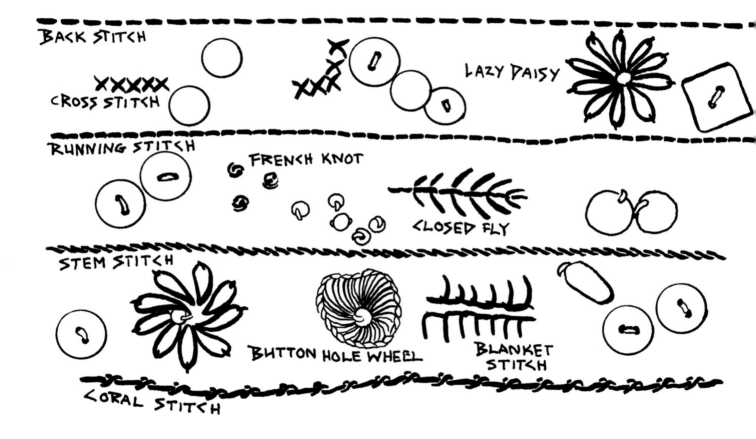

YOU WILL NEED

- Piece of silk
- Embroidery silk threads of different textures
- Embroidery needle
- Pearl buttons
- Various size pearls
- Picture frame
- PVA glue

SAMPLER

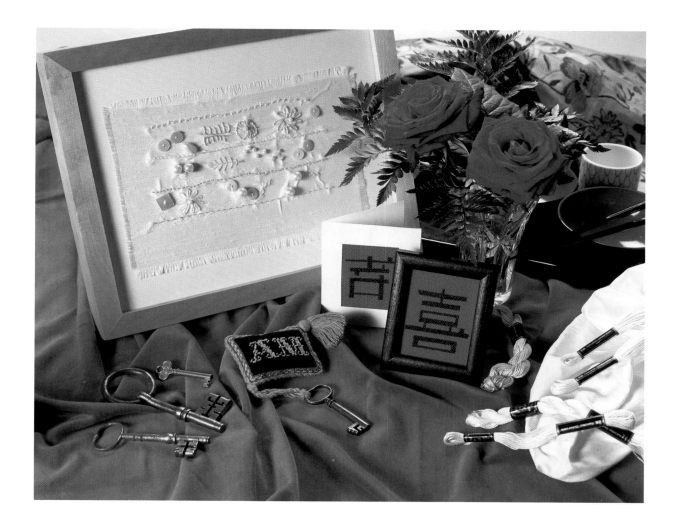

I love samplers and this is my modern version of what is the most traditional of needlecraft projects.

Add buttons and beads and experiment with whatever stitch you fancy

WHY STOP THERE!

From the useful to the simply decorative, embroidery can provide those small 'do-able' projects while sitting through the football on the TV!

PATCHWORK AND QUILTING

Patchwork is the piecing together of shaped bits of fabric. Quilting is the process of stitching together two layers of fabric with soft filler material between them to keep the stuffing evenly distributed - the stitching of this is often a decorative feature itself.

Real fans of these needle skills bring together patchwork, quilting and appliqué - probably not all in one evening mind you!

THE ORIGINS OF PATCHWORK AND QUILTING

Patchwork was very popular in medieval and renaissance Europe and its history is linked with that of quilting. Not only was it used to make and decorate ecclesiastical garments, but it was also applied to dresses and making material furnishings such as wall-hangings and bedcovers.

Quilting was known of in Persia as long ago as 490BC when garments made by quilting were used as armour at the battle of Marathon - presumably worn by the runners! Its use can also be traced in the rest of the Middle East, the Muslim areas of Africa, and India. It is China, however, where it is believed to have been invented. The Chinese made winter clothes from three layers of fabric and then used stitching to hold the middle layer in place.

In the Middle Ages knights coming back from the crusades brought home with them quilted undergarments used as underwear with their armour, and the idea soon took off in England. At first they were purely functional, for warmth, but gradually pieces were made using decorative techniques.

In the 14th century quilting bedcovers (quilts) were popular and by the 17th century they were both stylish and considered indispensable. Not only were they functional bedroom covers but some became very highly decorated and expensive.

Both patchwork and quilting developed considerably on transfer to America with the Pilgrim Fathers. These early settlers brought quilts from England but after some use they got worn and needed repairing, so they were mended with any piece of fabric that could be found, thus a form of patchwork quilting was born.

Obtaining cloth was a problem for the settlers, as England, frightened of losing its monopoly, would not export the new clothing technology. Initially, all the quilts were made of patchwork but as supplies of cloth improved and other materials became available, designs got more intricate, and appliquéd quilting became popular especially when its uses were extended to such things as petticoats and comforters.

In the early days patchwork quilting became a social pastime and neighbours would congregate and work together at gatherings known as 'quilting bees'. These social occasions, not only involved everybody helping to make quilts, but food would normally be supplied by the host and the party would end with dancing.

As the craft developed, quilting very often featured both appliqué and patchwork all in the one item and this type of work is considered to be of American origin.

A lot of quilting bees still exist today, and just like the olden days these groups of quilters often stitch significant quilts together to commemorate a wedding or perhaps some community event. I filmed a wonderful quilting bee in Devon a couple of years ago and I am convinced that there was more talking than sewing going on!

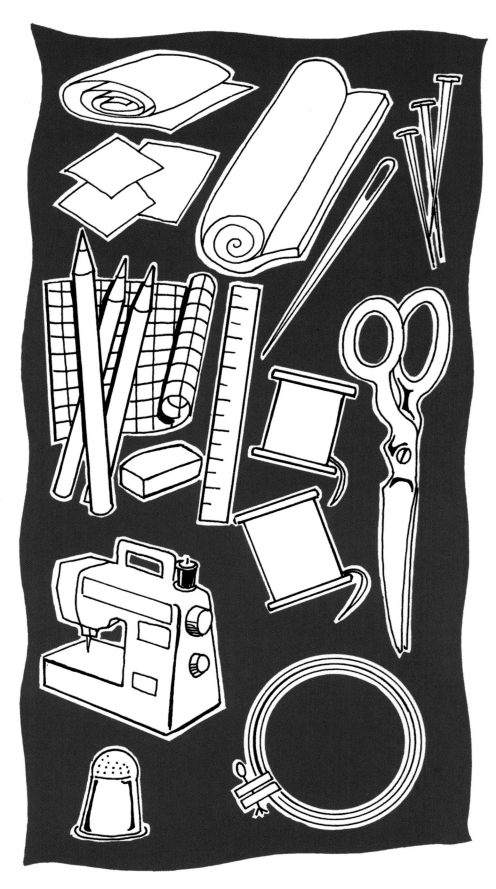

Material:

Background fabric
Contrasting material
Wadding
For designing:
Pencils
Graph paper
Rubber, ruler
Colouring pencils
Accessories:
Sewing machine
Thread for machine
Scissors
Pins
Needles
Thread
For quilting:
Quilting needle and thread
Frame or hoop

E Q U I P M E N T

The equipment you need for patchwork is the same as you would need for most sewing projects.

However, for quilting you may need, depending on the scale of your project, a **quilter's frame** or **hoop** as well as **quilting needles** and **quilting thread**. For the smaller projects like these in this book you can do without special equipment.

For both patchwork and quilting you will need certain drawing and sewing tools. For the designing and template making you will need **pencils, ruler, graph paper, colouring pens, protractors** and perhaps a **compass** for drawing circles.

Needles, thread, scissors and pins will be required, and don't forget a good fitting thimble to save the fingers.

When choosing your **fabrics and fillings** make sure that they are compatible in weight and similar as far as cleaning requirements are concerned.

Patchwork is a way of using up all those lovely bits of fabric that you can't bear to throw away but don't know what to do with.

Quilting, on its own or on top of patchwork, and appliqué can be both useful and decorative at the same time.

TECHNIQUES

PATCHWORK

The best tip I can give you is to stress yet again that the fabrics you use in your patchwork should be of similar type and weight. Dress cottons are perfect. Also, when choosing your thread select one that is a neutral shade that will sew all the different fabrics.

Another tip for machine patchworking is not to cut the thread between sections. Just pull a little out from the machine and sew the next sections together. In the end they will all hang together in one long strip and can be easily separated later. Do not press seams open, but instead press them all the same way to one side. Always iron on the wrong side first and then on the right side.

Squares are the most popular shapes to machine patchwork but you can use other shapes if you have more patience than I have. Hexagons, diamonds and scales are traditional shapes used in patchwork. Like cross-stitch it can be useful to plot out your pattern on graph paper first.

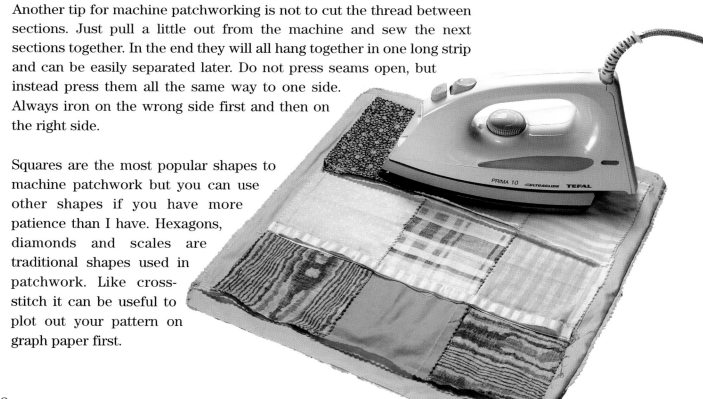

QUILTING

I have kept the quilting in this book to simple diagonals but you may feel inspired to create swirls, circles and other patterns with your running stitches. You can buy books of quilting patterns or create your own. Look for a suitable design and trace over it.

There is a technique called flat quilting where two layers of fabric are stitched together without a layer of wadding between them. The main use of this is to give weight to very fine fabrics.

You can stuff your quilted areas using a technique called trapunto. After the stitching is completed the backing fabric is cut and wadding inserted from behind so that the shape stands out in high relief. This can make quilting very warm.

STEP-BY-STEP

PATCHWORK

Now first of all, let me confess that the patchwork I suggest in this book is machine sewn. I really don't think you can complete a project in an evening by cutting out shapes and hand-stitching them, but by all means feel free to have a go if you are a speedy hand-sewer.

My instructions are to make a patchworked square the size of my cushion cover so you can reduce it or enlarge it as you wish. First, cut strips of fabric 12cm x 72cm from two contrasting pieces of material (A and B) and strips 12cm x 36cm from two other materials (C and D). Cut three individual squares 12cm x 12cm from fabric D, two from fabric A and one from fabric C. Then join the long edges of lengths A and B with a 1.5cm seam allowance and press the seams open. Cut across the joined piece at 12cm intervals. Do the same for lengths C and D.

Now just start arranging your patchwork strips and spare squares into the pattern you want. They will make a shape larger than you want with a zigzag edge (see my design on page 62). Sew all these together.

Now trim off the zigzags to get a straight-edged square and press. Then place the patchwork and backing material together with right sides facing and stitch all around leaving a 20cm gap for turning through. You will need to add your piping at this stage if you are using it.

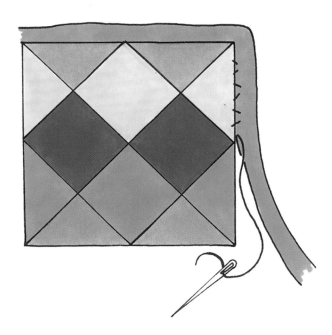

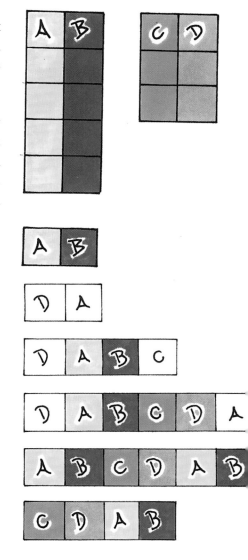

QUILTING

Like patchwork you can quilt by either machine or by hand. You need to choose a top piece of fabric and a backing piece, and then some wadding for the middle. Cut out the shape or size you want and place them together right sides showing with the wadding in between.

The stitch you use is a running stitch and the most important thing is to make sure it is evenly spaced and that the stitches are all the same length. Each stitch has to go through all the layers of the fabric. With hand-stitching it will help to get that sameness in stitches if you hold the needle vertical to the fabric.

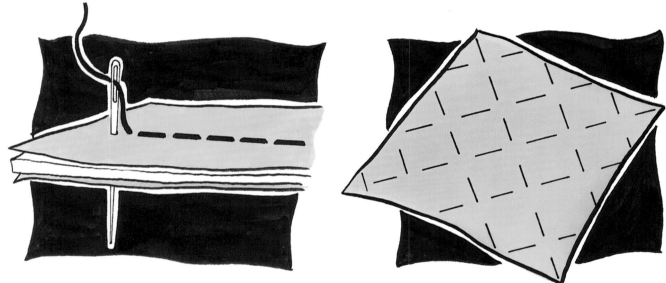

To machine quilt, first hand-tack your layers of fabric and wadding together with rows of long diagonal stitches.

For hand quilting use embroidery silks, which can either tone or contrast with the fabric.

Needlewise use a size 8 needle for hand-sewing and when machine-sewing use a needle suitable for the weight of fabric being quilted.

To finish your piece you need to bind or turn the edges in and stitch securely with more running stitches.

PATTERN

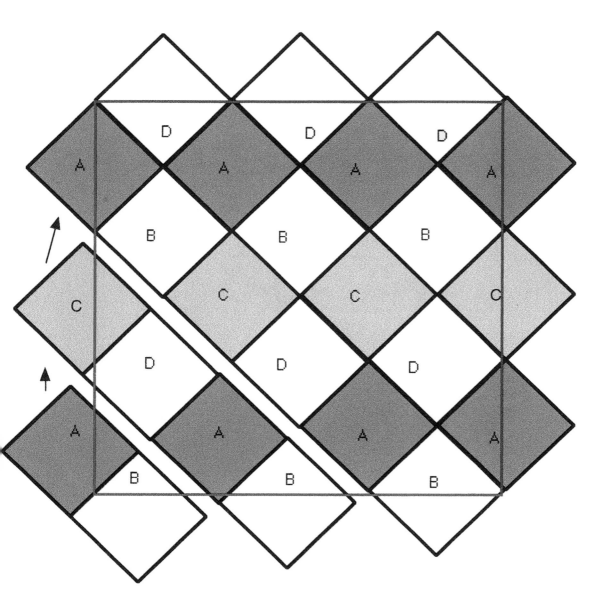

YOU WILL NEED

- Pieces of cotton material (all the same weight)
- Cotton fabric for cushion back
- Cotton
- Needle
- Piping – ready-made
- Cushion pad
- Scissors
- Piping foot for machine

Arrange and join strips into lengths and join them together as shown above. Rotate the piece and mark and stitch round the brown line as shown. Tack together the patchwork and backing with the right sides facing and stitch three sides. Trim and turn right side out. Insert cushion pad and stitch the opening closed. Stitch the trimming round the outer edge.

C U S H I O N

You can never have enough cushions in your home. Patchwork cushions are easily made from odd pieces of cloth - artistically arranged of course!

PATTERN

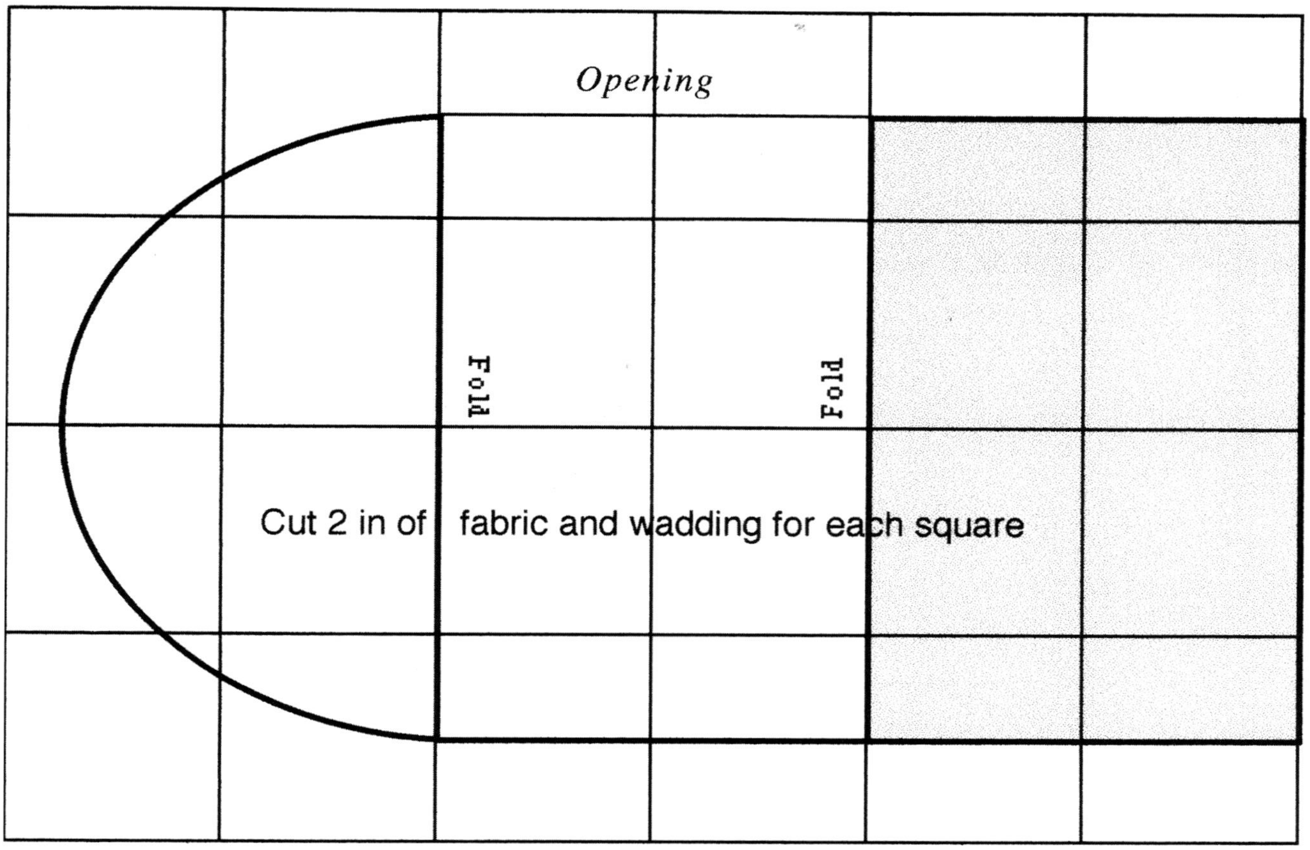

Opening

Fold

Fold

Cut 2 in of fabric and wadding for each square

YOU WILL NEED

- Pattern
- Needles
- Cotton
- Cord (for handle)
- Tassel

- Lining material
- Fabric
- Press fastener or Velcro
- Scissors

Cut one piece of the chosen material, quilting filling and lining material required to size using the pattern above. Place the quilting between the material and backing – right sides inside and sew together leaving an opening as shown. Turn the right side out and press. Fold over bottom (shaded area). Stitch together to form a pocket and add fastenings and cord.

E V E N I N G   P U R S E

Evening purses can cost a fortune for something that you will only use occasionally. Why not choose material to complement your outfit and quickly make one in the style and size you want at a fraction of the cost?

PATTERN

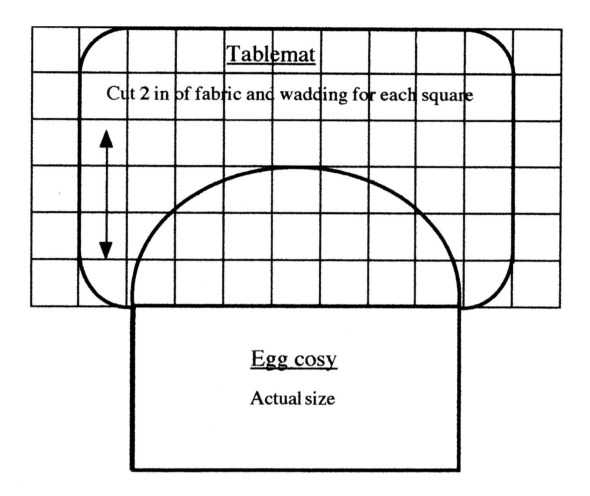

Tablemat

Cut 2 in of fabric and wadding for each square

Egg cosy

Actual size

YOU WILL NEED

- A copy of this pattern and graph paper
- Material – must be heatproof
- Padding
- Bias binding
- Cotton
- Scissors

Draw pattern full size on graph paper. Cut out two shapes in fabric and one in wadding. With wadding in between the fabric quilt vertically at 2 in intervals, trim edges and then bind.

To make cosy: Trace around the template onto a folded double thickness of fabric right side facing inwards. Stitch curved edges with a 1/4 in (6 mm) seam allowance. Turn the right way and trim with bias binding. Press.

TABLEMAT AND EGG

My youngest son, James, always has a boiled egg for breakfast, but the time between the egg being ready and him rushing around and getting to the table can be a bit elastic. This breakfast set is ideal and keeps his egg warm

WHY STOP THERE?

when patchwork and quilting can add colour and
comfort to so many items?

GLOSSARY

American crewelwork
In the 18th century in America crewelwork developed charact-eristics that were distinct from similar work in Europe. Designs were worked more sparsely and the motifs described indigenous fruit and flowers.

Appliqué
From the French verb 'to put on'. It is the sewing of patches to the surface of a material so they form a pattern either by their own shape and colour, or by the shape and colour of the ground material.

Band sampler
A narrow horizontal sampler with stitching in horizontal bands.

Berlin woolwork
It was a method of producing colourful work using charts made up of equal squares and each square represented one stitch.

Also saw the introduction of softer wools and aniline dyes.

Binca
An even-weave cloth

Bondaweb
A commercial iron-on web adhesive.

Canvas
A type of cloth woven in regular meshes and used as a basis for tapestry and embroidery.

Chenille
Velvety cord with pile all round used in trimming and bordering dresses and furniture.

Colour wheel
A diagram in the round showing the primary colours and the secondary colours that are formed from mixing the two adjoining primaries.

Couching
To embroider with gold thread etc. laid flat on the surface.

Crewel wool
A design worked in worsted on a ground of linen or cloth.

Even-weave fabric
A fabric where squares of threads are of equal size enabling stitches to be done by counting the threads.

GLOSSARY

Flat quilting
Where two layers of fabric are stitched together without a layer of wadding between them. The main use is to give weight to very fine fabrics.

Gauge
The number of threads that can be stitched to an inch.

Gold thread
Used in a variety of techniques especially couching.

Graph paper
Printed grids of equal size. Used to transfer and resize designs onto fabric.

Hoop
A round frame normally made of wood for stretching fabric on while it is stitched.

Needlepoint
A term used for embroidery worked on canvas.

Patterns
Decorative designs normally printed and used by embroiderers. Often in book form.

Piping
A thin pipelike length of folded cloth, often enclosing a fine cord.

Pouncing
To transfer a design to a surface by dusting a perforated pattern with pounce.

Sampler
A piece of embroider worked in various stitches as an example of skill.

Quilt
Two pieces of fabric plain, or sometimes formed from appliqué and patchwork stuffed with a layer of wool, cotton batting etc. and joined together with stitches.

Quilting bees
A social gathering for the purpose of making a quilt.

Trapunto
A kind of quilting in which the design is padded by pulling or cutting the threads of the underlying fabric to insert stuffing.

INDEX
OF PATTERNS

STITCHES

INDEX

E Q U I P M E N T
A N D
S U P P L I E R S

It wasn't so long ago that anyone interested in craft had to scour the back of specialist magazines to find the mail order outlets that stocked the materials and components needed. Either that or you hoped that the local haberdashery department or artists' materials shop might have it in stock.

Things are very different today. While many high street shops now stock craft materials, we've also got several large craft shop chains both in town centres and in out of town shopping malls. These massive 'sheds' have got very extensive ranges of stock and are also extremely competitive pricewise which is good news for the shopper.

I'm a great browser and often set off to buy a couple of small items only to return home with the essentials to start a whole new craft.

New products are being developed all the time to make craft easier, from new paints and clays to bigger and more imaginative ranges of blanks to decorate and embellish.

Alongside all the products you will often find details of courses and workshops in your locality and one thing that seems to be universal to all suppliers, from the local art shop, to the mail-order girl on the end of the phone to the person on the check-out till in the craft 'shed' is a shared enthusiasm to help you and me get the most out of our craft.

S U P P L I E R S

Manufacturers, Importers and Wholesalers

Atlascraft
4 Plumtree St
The Lace Market
Nottingham
NG1 1JL
For your local suppliers please call customer services :
Tel: 0115 9415280
Fax: 0115 9415281

A wide range of products covering most crafts. Main importers of Deka paints. Their range is available at John Lewis Partnership Shops.

ColArt Fine Art & Graphics Ltd
Whitefriars Avenue
Harrow
Middlesex
HA3 5RH

For your local suppliers please call customer services:
Tel: 0181 427 4343
Fax: 0181 863 7177

A large portfolio of well-known branded fine art materials including Winsor & Newton, Lefranc & Bourgeois and Dryad.

Philip & Tacey Ltd
North Way
Andover
Hampshire
SP10 5BA

For your local suppliers please call customer services :
Tel: 01264 332171
Fax: 01264 332226
E-Mail: sales@philipandtacey.co.uk

One of the longest established family firms in the arts and craft business.

Retail, Mail Order and Training Workshops

Cats Group
PO Box 12
Saxmundham
Suffolk
Tel: 01728 648717

Mail order specialist.

Creative World
The Bishop Centre
Bath Rd
Taplow
Berkshire
SL6 0NY
Tel: 01628 661331

These are one of the new expanding chains of larger shops. They carry thousands of lines covering all crafts. Good for browsing!

Quilting Bear
Whiteladies Rd
Clifton
Bristol BS8 2QY
Tel: 0117 923 8277

Mail order and a well-stocked shop. Has a strong American influence and an interesting proportion of their stock is imported from the U.S.

George Weill and Sons
The Wharehouse
Reading Arch Road
Redhill
RH1 1HG
Tel: 01737 778868
Fax: 01737 778894

A good general supplier who are known for their importing of the extensive Arty's cotton, silk and gutta collection and offer a full mail order service.

Nexus presents "Create It .....In an Evening", a series of books developed by Caroline Righton (your regular columnist on *Popular Crafts* TV presenter, producer, journalist and craft specialist), in response to the growing demand for innovative craft books suitable for today's busy lifestyle.

Other titles in this series

If you have enjoyed making the projects in this book, why not try your hand at other crafts? Other titles in this series include:

Create it with Paper in an Evening — Nine projects for making things with paper - découpage, papier mâché and hand-made paper. All are easily achievable by beginners with simple illustrated instructions and full colour throughout.

ISBN 1-85486-175-1

Create it with Paint in an Evening — Another nine easy projects for painting on silk, glass or fabric. Again split into three sections each one comprising an introduction, equipment list, techniques and a step-by-step guide to the basic skills needed.

ISBN 1-85486-174-3

Create it with Wax, Clay & Plaster in an Evening — Another nine easy to make projects using wax, clay and plaster. Again split into three sections each one comprising an introduction, equipment list, techniques and a step-by-step guide to the basic skills needed.

ISBN 1-85486-177-8

All the above titles should be obtainable from good bookshops. In the event of difficulty please contact the Books Division, Nexus Special Interests Ltd., Nexus House, Azalea Drive, Swanley, Kent BR8 8HU. Tel: 01322 660070

NEW TITLE FROM NEXUS SPECIAL INTERESTS

Alice and Daisy: Edwardian rag doll sisters to make and dress
Valerie Janitch

The basic Alice & Daisy dolls are simple enough for a beginner to make and equally easy to dress, with charming colour photographs that follow Alice & Daisy through their busy social diary. Whether it's lessons, shopping, tea in the country, a birthday party or just retiring to bed, an appropriate outfit is a necessity (plus beribboned underpinnings, of course!). Be warned! Once you have made the fashion conscious rag dolls, they won't allow you to resist the temptation to make their entire wardrobe. This book gives you the instructions to make the pretty and romantic Edwardian fashions that are such an important part of their sophisticated lifestyle. Alice & Daisy may be rag dolls, but *mere* rag dolls they are not!

To be published Autumn 1998.